TEAM LEADERS, I TOLD YOU SO'

Be The Best to Beat the Rest

INSPIRATION
VISION
MOTIVATION
INNOVATION
LEADERSHIP
TEAMWORK

SUCCESS

ALI ELFETURI

ISBN: Softcover   978-1-9845-9014-5
        EBook   978-1-9845-9015-2

To order additional copies of this book, contact:
Xlibris
0800-056-3182
www.xlibrispublishing.co.uk
Orders@ Xlibrispublishing.co.uk

CONTENTS

INTRODUCTION

In my 36 years of work experience, I have been promoted over the years for different leadership positions. I started out working on the shop floor as a young man as part of the production team, gained my qualifications as an electronic engineer and become part of the equipment engineering group. I was responsible for the day to day upkeep of the machines and after a number of years I took over the production team and became team leader. I can still remember the day I sat down with my manager for the interview. One of the questions I was asked was: "How are you going to manage the team and increase the activities within your shift?"

"Well," I replied, "I will spend time with the team and try to find out what we can do to achieve the required results and improve the performance of each member of the team." A few weeks later I got the job and met my team for the first time as a shift leader. Until that day, I was a member of the equipment engineer team and worked on fixing kits. As I progressed within the job, my responsibilities changed. I was still responsible for making sure the equipment was working with the help of the equipment group, and I was also responsible for the production group activities. This was my first challenge; to change the view of the team members and build trust in them. This way I could try to find the balance between the production team and engineering group.

I have written this book based on the experience I have gained over the last 37 years, and my aim is to share my knowledge and experience which may help anyone who wants to be a team leader.

Everything you read in this book is true, and you will see how leadership has changed over the past 37 years. I was hands on with my team, and kept a notepad with all the roles and responsibilities I had as team leader. This allowed me to measure myself and observe how I have progressed and developed over the years. It also enabled me to understand what my roles and responsibilities were, and what the expectations of the team were.

At the time when I got the job as team leader, I didn't have the experience to lead a team of employees to carry out the job and to achieve set goals. However, what I did have was the motivation and work ethic which helped me in achieving my ambition.

So, to do the job I started by observing others, who at the time were known as supervisors. Their job is to achieve targets in any way they can, and success rate in the role was based on number of years' experience in the department. As I started to put my team together, I thought about how I could strive for the best within my team, without getting frustrated and annoyed with them. As we all know, in any job we will always come across conflict, and believe me I have certainly come across this in my time. I found it difficult to deal with employees who had the "it's my way or the highway" viewpoint.

So, over the following years I tried to use different skills and strategies to manage my staff. At one time, I had over 48 employees working on rotating 12 hour shifts, every one of them with a different idea of the word "team."

After 5 years as team leader, and as part of the staff development, the company had arranged for all the senior staff to attend leadership training courses which were held once a month and lasted for 12 months. The classroom training was fine, but nothing can compare with the experience you learn during dealing with people every day in the department. Every day is different, people have good days, bad days, good attitudes, days where they are willing to give 100%, and days where their thoughts are preoccupied with something happening at home. All these factors can affect their performance, behaviour and attitude. As a team leader, your role is to get the best out of your team, in a professional way. This did not come without difficulties.

You can have all the qualifications to qualify for the job, but nothing can beat the experience you learn over the years, and the value that comes from dealing with people on a daily basis.

In this book I have covered everything you need to know to become a team leader, section leader and group leader. Regardless of your job type, here you will learn the core skills and attributed required to make the most out of your team as an excellent team leader.

SECTION "1"

Leadership

The definition of leadership is the ability to lead, inspire and motivate a group of people to carry out jobs in a professional way, with the end result in mind. It could be manufacturing, armed forces, healthcare; a team leader will always be needed. Effective leadership is based upon ideas and needs to achieve the final results. Every job may have different specifications and different needs, but those ideas, ambitions and instructions need to be communicated to all members of your team. They need to be communicated in a way that engages them enough to act as the business requires. The job as a team leader or a line manager is not just about leading a team of people, it's about making the correct and sound (and sometimes difficult) decisions. Creating and articulating a clear vision and direction with the ability to sell that vision to the teams, allows you to establish achievable goals, providing the team with the training and tools necessary to achieve those goals.

No team leader or line manager can achieve the skill of a strong leader, with paper qualifications alone. A good attitude, team work and self-drive is much more important than a degree. I have found this out for myself over the years, as I had to change the way I managed my team. Life experience is the best way to learning these kinds of skills because external pressures outside the workplace is a large contributor to work stress, and can put people under extreme stresses. This can push the individual to the point of breakdown or leaving the job altogether, and that's why it is important to take a step back and remain calm and professional in these situations. This is a key skill to have as a manager.

Being respectful doesn't just benefit you; it benefits everyone around you. I found that when it comes to getting the commitment, engagement and the motivation from my team, in order to achieve the required results for the business. As a team leader I needed to demonstrate respect to everyone around me, not only my manager but all the people involved in getting the job done. Respect is important for the employer and employee. There's no use shouting, losing your temper, and raising your voice as you won't achieve the desired results. Don't favour one team member any more than the other, this will destroy the respect and can lead to employees feeling victimised or discriminated against. Don't get me wrong, there is the occasion where you will need to make adaptations for your employees and attend to certain employees more than others, but you can still treat all your staff with the same values and respect. If for any reason, a member of staff is not meeting the basic requirements of the job, ensure you have followed your company's procedure and inform Human resources. This way you are protecting not only the employee but yourself too.

Always treat everyone fairly, have the same set of expectations for every team member and create team rules that you expect everyone to respect and follow, setting clear expectations upfront, including clear roles and responsibilities.

In an interview for any role or position, the interviewee will be expected to meet the required job description. Some people come across well in interviews, whilst others crumble and forget everything they've ever learnt. More importantly when the new starter joins the team, the team leader should be clear about that individual's role is within their new team. This will allow for a smooth integration into the team, and ensure each team member has a good level of understanding around their expected performance.

Leadership is not about being liked by your team and managers, as you will be judged by the results you and your team achieves. People favour the leader before they favour the vision. Leaders create an atmosphere of trust, and must recognise that trust is earned. Successful teams are confident, trusted, and supported by their leader.

Strong leaders build strong teams and a group of people who work together rather than individually, are able to adapt their style to suit any given situation or workplace crisis. As a team leader, it is important to recognise your strengths and weaknesses. You should acknowledge the strengths and weaknesses within your team and focus on developing the weaknesses and praising the strengths. The team will flourish and deliver the required results.

One of my weaknesses in my early days as a team leader is that I did not delegate some of my responsibilities to other members of the team. At the time, I felt that completing the job myself would be quicker, and I didn't necessarily trust the skills of others to complete the job for me. As I progressed in my role, I realised that I needed to trust my team to do a good job, and I learnt to delegate to others and started to see positive results. In turn, this enabled my staff to build their trust within me.

Trust leads to loyalty, and loyalty leads to people striving to do their best to deliver results for you and the company. We all know that to earn trust and respect we have to give trust and respect, if you do this within your team there will be no limit to what you and your team can achieve.

Your team will succeed when there is a good level of communication, encouragement of ideas and innovations, and openness for feedback and discussion. Some work places have "improvement teams" which are designed to specifically work on finding improvements within the team and within the products and services provided. The team should be made up of operators who are on the front line of the production, as they can shed light on the everyday issues and advise best on a course of action in improving the situation. The other part of the team should be made up of engineers and managers who can support in improvement in productivity, cost reduction, and increasing output. The output of the meeting should then be communicated to everyone across the company. This will link channels between all teams.

One of the problems the team can face is that the engineering team or the process owner sees themselves as the champion of the process as they have developed and made the process. They may be reluctant to accept any changes, which may impact on the quality of the process. The team need to work together, and insist on looking for a better way to improve the states que, even if the process owner makes it difficult to do so. I will refer back to this during the conflict section of the book.

We are human and we all make mistakes! If your team member makes a mistake or fails to perform as per the process specification, which results in the termination of production, then as a team leader you will hold some responsibility. As team leader, it is really important to highlight problems or mistakes and learn from them as a team. Turn the problem into a learning opportunity and it may prevent it from occurring again.

When I was an apprentice, my teacher said to me; "an intelligent person learns from their mistakes but a wise person learns from other people's mistakes." That has stuck with me for all these years, not just in work but in all aspects of life. If someone makes a mistake in the workplace, don't be happy that it wasn't you, but use it to your advantage and learn from the mistake that was made.

As a team leader or line manager you should have the skills to inspire and motivate your team. If you are self-motivated with enthusiasm and a positive attitude, you can energise your team to achieve difficult goals and increase the level of performance from everyone in the team. Many team leaders and line managers usually focus on accomplishing tasks in their job descriptions while forgetting to inspire and motivate their team. In my view, this is a big mistake. I found when the focus is to inspire, we can unlock a high level of additional effort and energy from members of the team. This will determine success or failure. Every team leader needs to find ways of inspiring their team to get the best possible performance out of the team. I found over the years that most people want to achieve a better level of performance, but they need help and someone to aspire to see them succeed. I have seen a number of people achieve their ambition by pushing themselves, and with the help from their team leader they have improved within their work role.

A team leader should be optimistic in order to succeed and successfully carry a team. *"A pessimist sees the difficulty in every opportunity; an optimist sees the opportunity in every difficulty." (Winston Churchill)*.

An optimistic leader should always look for an opportunity even in a difficult situation. He or she should never quit even if the situation going against the plan. It's important for the team leader to have this quality as it will boost the team morale and allow the team to work positively towards the common goal. A successful leader is always looking for ways to improve, they recognize that they're never perfect, and there's always room for improvement. To be a successful leader you should be always working to improve your skills. As a team leader I always pushed myself to improve in my job. I had an ambition from the first day I started as an operator, to get up the ladder and move up to the next level, which meant I had to work harder than some of my colleagues. I never accepted that doing the basic job was enough to get by. I was continually looking at improving myself, attending college in the evenings after 8 hour shifts, and revising and looking for new learning in any spare time that I had. This enabled me to improve my qualifications which helped me to become an electronic engineer. The point is that you just have to have an ambition and try to achieve it. You will get help but you need to have an aspiration and ambition to get there.

As a leader you need to have a passion for winning. In other words, getting by is never good enough. During my experiences over the last 37 years as a team leader, I have always wanted to win. I have always wanted the best, and will continue to want the best and achieve targets I have set myself. I want to produce the best team within the company, and bring out the best in others. Think about the role of a football manager. These respected clubs look for a manager with lots of experience and a passion for winning. They need a manager who is passionate, and willing to project this passion onto their team. Some managers don't have this passion, and you can see this when his team start to lose the game. They give up and crumble after one error or mistake. Personally, I can't understand this and think if you believe in something you should work on it and learn from any mistakes that are made. I'll give you an example. Manchester City won the Premiere league for the first time in 44 years. They scored the winning goal in the last few minutes of the game. The score was level prior to this. If the team, managers, players and entourage would have given up and chosen not to give 110% effort until the very end, they would not have won. But they really believed they could, so they kept giving their best performance right up until the last whistle was blown.

I know from my experiences as team leader, that the job can often be lonely; you are constantly making decisions, many of which upset people, but as long as you do it in a calm way then you are doing a good job. My advice is to try to make your job fun and enjoyable as this will help to reduce your stress levels. You need to enjoy the daily challenge as there is no point coming to work with a negative attitude. We spend more time at work than home so you need to look on the positive side of things and enthusiasm about what you can achieve during your working hours,be positive and upbeat even when things going wrong .

It's no coincidence that most of the successful leaders and managers tend to be of a more mature age. You can never underestimate the value of experience. Whichever company you work for, they all send their younger members of staff on training courses to expand their knowledge and experience of the job. One thing they can't teach is man-management. This is the main ingredient which all leaders need in order to succeed; you can only achieve this through experience.

The one thing I will tell every team leader is that you will never please everyone. They may not like you at that moment in time, but they will respect your decisions. It is better to be respected than liked. You will never be liked by everyone as you may have over 50 employees reporting to you. It is impossible for you to keep everyone happy and be a good manager at the same time. This is part of your responsibility, to accept this and work through it as a manager. I have seen and experienced this in great depth over the 37 years I have worked as an engineer and a team leader.

People talk about the stress they get from doing their jobs, and there are jobs which come with big responsibility and lots of pressure. In most manufacturing jobs you will see or may see and experiences like I did. Some of these stresses and pressures are created by ourselves, as a lot of the time we are poor at planning and also poor at managing our time. Planning and the use of time-management is one of the most important ingredients in order to be a good team leader. Stress in most jobs comes because we can't achieve the results required for the business, this could be due to a number of things; promising customers things that cannot be achieved, poor quality merchandise, lack of staffing etc. All these things can impact on management stress, as they are trying to achieve their target and can see the hard work their staff are putting in. Sometimes these issues may be out of the manager's control. Different jobs come with different stressors, for example; Doctor's face high levels of stress on a daily basis, as they deal with people's lives. One mistake could result in a catastrophe. They have to focus with a clear mind all the time, on top of working long hours, sometimes without a break, and with poor staffing levels. They are underpaid for the service they provide but have to carry on anyway. Even with any emergency services it can be highly stressful, think about the police force who are putting their life on the line on a daily basis. The same goes with the fire department. Think about Gordon Ramsay. He is always so stressed, as he is passionate about delivering quality food to his paying customers. That's why he is successful and achieves delicious food. He has high standards and expects everyone else to be the same.

Across all kinds of jobs we all have responsibilities to achieve set goals and to be the best at our job. With the guidance and help from others who are experienced in the job, we can achieve our goals and strive to be better leaders. As much as it is important to have the right qualifications, I firmly believe that experience plays a bigger part in achieving a good standard of leadership, which will help people along their way to becoming a good leader.

There are plenty of books and information available to everyone, and most Universities run courses on how to become a good team leader or manager. You will still need lots of experience to become a good team leader, and I would recommend for anyone who wants to be a leader to spend time on the shop floor or in the front line. This will give you the opportunity to see and experience things which are not in any books. There are plenty of examples of good leaders and mangers, who started and learned their skills when they were on the shop floor. Take a look at some of the famous football managers. Alex Ferguson set an example for his team, learned the value of hard work, and discipline and determination paid off.

Ferguson was always the first on the training ground every morning he expected extremely high standards of discipline and character from his players. Whether they were youth players or superstars, he didn't just focus on their skills; he wanted to ensure they had the character, ambitions and determination to maximize their talents and then become winners. He gained all his experiences during working at Aberdeen Football club as a manager, and he set a clear standard on what he wanted from his team. They all worked extremely hard, and he manged to sell his ideas and convinced them that they could become the champions of the Scotland and they did. He did not accept that victory just came from talent, but that it came from hard work, persistent effort and determination. When he took over Manchester United as a manager he continued with his high standards from day one, and within few years his team started to dominate the English football league, and they became the champion of England. During his time at the club, they had over 25 years of successes and a number of players flourished and became household names while playing for Manchester United. Similarly, the success of any team or organization cannot merely rest on natural ability or talent, you can have the best engineers in the world but if they don't have the self-motivation to get up and work hard and give that little extra, then their goals will not be achieved.

Take a look at Karen Brady. What a great leader in business and a fantastic business woman. In her books, she talks about her values which led her to success; *"I started in a very junior role at Saatchi & Saatchi on its graduate scheme, even though I was 18. While I only had A-levels and a bunch of GCSEs, I had my core values and they were the key to being successful. I had integrity and an enthusiasm to work; I was hungry to get on. These are the same values I have today."*

As you can see from these examples of leadership, it is all about setting examples for others to follow. If you have determination to be successful then you will achieve your goals. The key is to lead by example and it's really important that your team see you leading by an example, and that you show a huge amount of dedication, determination, good communication and positive thinking.

To have that dream team in any business, the organization needs to have a great team leader. It doesn't matter which working sector it is, it could be the emergency services, the army, manufacturing, health care and service sector, all they need to have is a good team leader or a good line manager. That can only come with experience and training which is very important to achieve the required results. A great team will also depend on the environment the work place can provide. It will also depend on the quality of the training available and the adaptability of managers to their staff. Some individual's learn at slower paces than others, but as long as you can see that someone has the skills to be a good communicator, a team player, and a self-motivated individual.

SECTION "2"

Line Manager/Team Leader

Over the years it has proven time and time again, that the team leader is one of the most vital yet underestimated positions in any company and in all working places regardless of the business type. The team leaders in these positions act as the middle link between their teams and the rest of the organisation, and this will apply to all types of job. In this position there are huge conflicting pressures between the needs of the business and work force. The organization wants the business to be very successful, whilst on the other hand the work force has plenty of issues which can have an impact on achieving the business targets. The team leaders or the line mangers must achieve the organization results regardless of the issues and the problems occurring on a daily basis. In these positions, the team leader will be looked on by his team member as their champion – their spokesperson – whose role it is to champion their ideas and work issues. As a team leader you have responsibilities and obligations to your team, and you may find yourself working as psychologist I disguise. You need to understand the individual team member's behaviours, and what impacts on their mood, anger levels, work performance. Dealing with people is one of the most difficult jobs. Especially if you have a large group of people reporting to you, people of different beliefs, backgrounds and behaviours.

Team leaders, line managers and section leaders all do the same and all have the same responsibilities. Just some companies like to use the name of 'line manager' for their front-line team leaders. There is however a difference between line managers and department managers. The difference between the team leader and department manager is that team leaders are involved in creating, directing, leading and compelling visions of the future and the development for their team. They then communicate that vision, and help people understand and commit to it. Department managers, on the other hand, are responsible for ensuring that the vision and the development of the team are implemented efficiently and successfully. The department managers are responsible for the department finances and setting the cost of the development of the staff. Both of these jobs are linked together and usually each one depends on the other and, to be successful in achieving the organization targets, both team leader/line managers and department managers have to work together. There is no point motivating your team to work towards the vision of the future if you fall flat on your face when it comes to implementations. If the team leader and department manager fail to deliver on their promises, it can be very disappointing. I have seen disappointed people when their vision and hard work completed on a project, may not have been implemented. They usually give up and decided not to get involved in any further improvement ideas. They feel let down and demotivated. Not all projects and ideas can be implemented, which is why as a team leader or a line manger you should focus on the one vision or project you can implement.

'You're either born a leader or you're not', this is what most people believe, but life experience tells us a different story. Not everyone can be a leader and not everyone has the skills to be a good leader, but in some specific cases some people are born to be a leader. I also believe that some people are born with certain merits that help them to be leaders, and some people need to learn the skill to be a good leader, but both types of people can improve their skills to become a good leader.

A large part of the role of a team leader is telling other people what to do and how to do it. This is, however, far from being an easy task as not only do you need to consider what to say, but also the way to say it, and when to say it. In some jobs, such as the emergency services, these instructions given by the team leader can be the difference between life and death. Everyone has been in the position where they have given a simple instruction and been amazed to see it wildly misinterpreted. Just remember these kinds of instruction can save people's lives in some jobs. Take the example of the doctor when they give their instruction to their team during an operation; one wrong error in communication can result in the loss of life. Often, we put this down to the fact that they must be 'uneducated' or they mustn't 'understand', but it can just be poor communication from your leader. Rarely do we address the real reason, which is that we didn't make the instruction clear.

As a team leader, you have a big challenge in front of you. You need to be able to transfer visions and ideas into action. To create the climate in which your team can turn challenging opportunities into remarkable success, and not just all about success for the organization, is also about providing opportunities and support for the individual to achieve their goals and ambitions. The way to achieve these is to inspire a shared vision and to challenge the present process. This will enable and motivate others to act and work towards the new vision. The more people that are committed, the more effective they are in influencing others.

One of the things I have experienced over the years is that people who are committed are the ones who don't give up. They always end up achieving their ambitions and getting the reward they deserve. They usually set an example for those who don't have the confidence or the experience, and create an environment where your team and working staff can develop and improve their skills.

From my experience, people usually look to the leader of the group or their team leader for inspiration and commitment. Always try to show how much you are committed and inspired to the job/vision/projects you are working on, then it will show in your attitude and actions. Your team will watch and see how you act and they will follow your lead. You have to be the force to drive changes and help others to accept that the present process could change to achieve better results.

As a team leader you will need to have a positive attitude and be self-motivated. These factors can go a long way in your work place to help your team. Don't dwell on negativity and always aim to be positive. If something doesn't quite go to plan, this will help in creating positive attitudes and a healthy work place environment, even during busy and stressful periods. If you are a positive leader and have not demonstrated any negative attitudes, this will help raise the morale amongst your team members. If your team feel that they work in a positive environment, they will be more likely to work hard and increase productivity. As a team leader you are part of a team or a group, but at the same time you may feel like the lone voice and the main driver. You have to remember it's the team leader's responsibility to see the end goal and vision of the company and to lead others towards it. When others do not see it the same way you have to be the lone voice to bring them back on track.

There are plenty of ways to find out what kinds of skills your team have. Not the skill to operate machines or carry out the daily jobs, I am talking about the other skills; skills such as being a good team player, a good communicator, a good listener. Some of them may be good at communicating, some may be very good at listening, and others may be good leaders in their own way. So, to find out the different types of skills my team may have, I decided to get my team together and split them into a number of smaller groups to complete the 'egg drop game.'

The egg drop is about supplying the teams with materials to build a contraption around the egg that will keep the egg from breaking when dropped from the first or second floor in the building. The aim of the game is to prevent the egg from cracking.

I supplied the teams with the following: 10 sheets of newspapers, bubble wrap, rubber bands and the raw egg. The items vary in price. The prices are displayed on the items to see if the employees could save the egg from breaking whilst also being cost efficient. The teams have 30 minutes to complete the task.

As the teams get together and read the instructions, they begin to work on protecting the egg with the materials they have. Each egg is then tested to see which one survives. Some of my other colleagues who are also team leaders are observing the employees during this task. They are looking at their ability to lead the team, plan the task, complete the task, communicate with the rest of their team, and their ability to problem solve the task. In my experience, I have found that this activity will rely heavily on team work, problem solving and leadership skills. Some team members might stand out and be proactive, getting themselves involved while others may just stand back and watch.

This kind of task gives me the ideas and the information I need to understand the strengths and weaknesses of my team members. With that information I could then put together a development program to suit the individual to work on developing their weaknesses and perfecting their strengths.

The objectives and desired outcomes from completing this task are:
- Co-operation
- Creative thinking
- Planning
- Teamwork
- Time management
- Communication
- Active listening
- Conflict resolution
- Leadership

When the game has been completed, it can be useful to ask the individual's the following:
- What have you learned from this game?
- Have you achieved the objective of saving the egg?
- Would you do anything different if you had a second chance?
- How does this game relate to your job role?

As a team leader I have learned a lot about my team from these kinds of games, as it helps people come out of their shell and become comfortable with being part of a team. As we all know, not everyone is proactive and outgoing. Some individuals are quiet and find it difficult being part of a team until they feel comfortable in their own environment.

Over the years, I have come across plenty of instances where people did not want to be part of a team due to a number of reasons. Some of them had difficulties mixing with other members of the team, some had communication issue due to language barriers, and some found it difficult interacting within a social environment. Over time, most of these individuals have become part of one team or another and felt happy with their surroundings and their colleagues. I have experienced these issues myself, as I felt isolated when I first arrived in this country as a student; I did not speak the language and it was very difficult to mix with others who were of a different background or culture to myself. Over the years, I have learnt to speak the language and communicate with others around me. I felt this was important in order to be part of the team and integrate into the society we live in. Feeling isolated can lead to feelings of anxiety, rejection, and low mood related to the workplace.

SECTION "3"

Leadership Behaviour

Human behaviour can be very different from one person to another in the work place and also outside of work. Here's an example; during my holiday in Florida, the infamous ash cloud struck on the last day of our holiday. My family and I were instructed by our airline to report to the airport on time. As we arrived at the check in desk, we were told that no flights would be leaving for over 36 hours, and that we should go back to the hotel. What happened next made me think about the poor behaviours of others, and what can impact on how a person behaves. This poor girl at the check in desk was attempting to explain the reasons for the delay, however people were pushing and shoving, screaming and shouting, and not accepting of an answer. People didn't consider that there safety was the main reason for the delay, and their tempers and emotions were getting in the way of behaving rationally. My family and I went back to our villa, and we arranged to stay for another 3 days until the ash had cleared and we could get home safe. In my job as a team leader, I experience and see so many different and difficult behaviours from people, and I have to analyse the individual team member's behaviour. The reason for that is to try to understand any abnormal behaviour and to see if any underlying issues are causing the unusual behaviours. These abnormal behaviours can affect the individual team members which can have an impact on the individual and the team performance.

Some of the abnormal individual behaviour can be caused by issues occurred outside of work. Problems at home can change the person's behaviours during working hours, as people cannot focus on the job due to these problems. Some people don't like talking about their life outside of work, but as a team leader you will see that their normal behaviours can become abnormal and their performance may drop. In my experience, the only way to help that individual is to give them time and let them know that if they want to talk you are there to listen. Don't comment or give any advice unless they ask for your opinion. An example of something to say is; ''I have noticed that you're not performing at your usual best, is there anything I can do to help?''

At that point they may open up and start to talk about the issues. In this section we will look at how the team leader should set their own behaviours and set an example on how to lead their teams and gain their respect and trust. This is a key skill to be a successful leader and it doesn't matter which environment or types of business you work in, this will apply to all kinds of industries. To have a successful team you will need to respect your team and trust them to do the job. It's fine to be part of your team and have a laugh with them, but you need to know when to draw the line and take a step back and let them get on with the job. As you can see from the following example, this is what can happen when a member of the team becomes the leader of the team.

A famous football club decided to sack the manager and replace him with one of the players. The new manager was part of the team and continued to maintain his relationships with the players. He continued socialising with them outside of work and enjoyed going for a few drinks with them. He soon discovered that his players weren't arriving on time for training, and didn't respond to his instructions on the playing field; this resulted in the team losing their games and the team ultimately were relegated.

This is just one example of how the team leader did not take a step back and set the standards and the expectations he wanted from his team to achieve better results.

This can apply to any job, and when a member of a team is promoted to team leader, they will need to take a step back and manage the team. It can be difficult to start with, especially if you have close friendships with some members of your team. When you are in the work environment, you have to manage and treat your team members like everyone else reporting to you. You must be seen to be fair and have the same respect and trust for everyone.

I have experienced this myself when I was part of a work based football team. Some of the players were my employees, and thought it was okay to behave in the same way at work as on the football field; arriving late, taking extended lunch breaks and so on. At the beginning, I found it difficult to deal with, but over the following months I found the confidence to speak with them and set boundaries. It is important to set the standard;

"In work I am the team leader and you should accept and respect that." This worked well for me and I haven't experienced any issues regarding this since.

The leader must be very clear about what they want from their team, and must set a clear and achievable goal. You must become the change you want to see in your team, and it is often said that 'actions speak louder than words,' but how often do we actually walk the walk?

How can we expect others to change if we aren't ready to change ourselves?

To motivate the team, you need to start by seeing yourself as a role model and as an example to others.

As a team leader I spend lots of time with my team on the shop floor. This enables me to understand their behaviour during work time, and allows me to build some understanding of how each individual works. What motivates them? I always try to make myself available to answer any questions, and as a team leader you need to have those self-motivating attributes in order to influence your team. Your team will follow in your footsteps therefore it is important to lead by example.

On the other hand, if you're a team leader that likes to work away in the office away from your team, it is important to consider that you may lose regular contact with your team, and this may impact on your relationships with your colleagues as a team leader. You must have regular contact with your team, not just once a day, but frequently enough in order to coach your team to be successful. We don't see the football coach training his team without being on the front line with them. In Hong Kong, one of the best restaurants is based in one of the five star hotels, and the head chef has over 30 chefs reporting to him. He spends most of his time in the kitchen with his team. He doesn't physically engage with cooking, but he advises and observes the food leaving the kitchen. He ensures it is of a high standard and meets the customer's expectations. He motivates his team and supports them from the very front, not from an office down a corridor. He ensures the standards don't drop, and if they do, he is there to support and guide his team in taking appropriate action. All team leaders or line managers should spend 75% of their time on the front line with their team.

In one of my previous roles, I worked for a retuned goods company. I was part of a team responsible for operating the mail bags on the shop floor. There were 15 members on our team, all working for one supervisor. We only saw him on a Friday afternoon when he brought our weekly wage slips.

I was shocked to learn that our supervisor did not know the names of his team members, to the point where another team member had to introduce him to his own team. Some of the team members had been there for over 5 years and he was still unaware of their names. Some team leaders may feel this is not important, but in my opinion, this is one of the most important things a team leader can do. A team leader should make the effort to learn not only their employee's names, but also about them as a person, their background, religion and culture. If you, as a leader, have a good relationship with your team, they will respect you for showing an interest and in not just the work they do, but them as an individual. If you take a look at some of the most successful companies around the world, I can guarantee their team leaders are based on the shop floor, where team members can approach them for support and guidance.

A good leader sets a high standard of accountability for themselves and their employees, and as a team leader you are responsible for both the successes and failures of your team, therefore, you must accept blame when something does go wrong. If your team see their leader pointing fingers and blaming others, they will lose respect for their leader. The better thing to do here is to accept mistakes and failures, and then devise clear solutions for improvement. Remember that before you motivate your team, be sure to motivate yourself. Be the sort of person others can get behind and support and that will earn you lots of respect from your team.

Your team member needs to be able to feel comfortable coming to you with questions and concerns. It is important for you to demonstrate your integrity — your team will only trust leaders they respect. By being open and honest, you will encourage the same sort of honesty in your team. Remember that people need to feel respected and appreciated in order to stay focused and committed to the team. This is important but not always easy to sustain. Commitment and respect is the key for any team to be successful in their objectives and achievement.

In this job you need to learn and how to deal with pressure. It's one of the most important skills in this job as you will experience pressure and need to know how to manage it. You are responsible for your team and the people that report to you. Situations will occur which are out of your control, and you need to know how to deal with it in professional and calm way.

Team leaders are the focal point of the team and their fundamental responsibility is to lead from the front. Consistency is the key to great leadership; consistency of behaviours, performance and expectations. Trust leads to loyalty and loyalty leads to people doing their best to deliver results for you and the company. To earn trust and respect you have to give trust and respect, as well as look out for your people. If you do, there will be no limit to what you can achieve.

There are a number of common behaviours recognised in an effective team leader in charge of any type of production team or service provider:
- Clear and effective communication
- Recognising the developmental requirements of team members and executing plans in achieving these developments
- Ability to set goals and motivate team members
- Providing enthusiastic and creative encouragement, and rewarding the people involved
- Acting as a role model and leading by example

Examples of poor communicator and leadership Behaviours

Case study

This incident occurred during a professional football game a number of years ago. The team were losing 4-0 at half time and the manager of the club lost his temper, deciding to keep his players on the field at half time rather than using this time to group with his team in private. He criticised his team about their poor performance, and singled out players in an aggressive manner. However, he forgot to remove his headset before unleashing his anger, meanwhile 37,000 spectators listened in on his gruelling telling off. He lost the players and supporters respect, and there was little confidence in him as a manager following this point. A few points for you to consider;

- As a team leader do you think the manager chose the correct place to confront his team?
- Would you do the same if a member of your team on the shop floor underperformed or missed their target? You should always conduct this kind of conversation in a private environment.
- How should he have addressed his concerns? He should have waited until the team were in their dressing room.
- What does this behaviour tell us about the team leader? It demonstrates that the manager has lost control of his team and is unable to implement a strategy to influence their performance.
- What effect does this kind of behaviour have on the team and the individual? It can reduce morale and prevent you from achieving your desired target.
- What impact will this behaviour have on the club (company)? They will lose their supporters and potential company loss orders.

I know from my experience over the years that dealing with people is a difficult job, but with years of experience as a team leader you can handle most difficult situations. Always try to be clam and never shout across the shop floor at any of your team members. Conflicts are never resolved through angry confrontations – this only adds fuel to the fire. Always choose the correct time and place to have a private conversation with the individual.

Understanding Poor Behaviours

It's important to deal with individual examples of bad behaviour, but it's also very important to understand the root cause. If a team member keeps making mistakes and tries to cover them, then we need to look to why this happening. Is this a sign of a 'blame' culture that leaves team members afraid to be honest? In a case like this we must try to understand the real reason. Is more training required? Is the workload too much for the individual? Or are the physical or mental needs of the person impacting on the person's ability to complete the task? Are the hours too long? Rotating shifts may not suit everyone and there are plenty of working environmental issues which can lead to poor behaviours and performance. At the same time we need to try to understand and investigate any underlying issues when people are routinely phoning in sick. Is it the same person? Is it long term sickness? Or is it due to other reasons? Team leaders and line managers, with the help of the human resources, must work together in underpinning any issues with stress and workload. All departments need to look at all issues with regards to poor behaviours and try to understand the problem. Then they need to speak to the individual about their behaviours and try to find the reason as to why they behave like that. It may be due to an issue outside of work, which can cause some people to behaviour very poorly. While they are in work they may want to be left alone for a period of time, and that can be the best way to get them back on track.

Normal and abnormal behaviours

Personal distress can be due to many things. It could be due to issues at home which can add to work pressures and can affect the individual's normal behaviour. This then becomes abnormal behaviour and as a team leader you should be able to see the difference in your team. We have to remember that circumstances affect people behaviours; you need to be able to understand these kinds of problems and how to deal with it. Over the years I have seen many examples of these abnormal behaviours. Some people don't like to talk about their home life and the problems they have, but their behaviour will change and their performance will slow down. That is the time, as a team leader, when you need to be acting as a psychologist. Your actions can help to ease the personal problem for that individual during working time, and you must do all that you can to support them as much as you are able. Human behaviour is very difficult to understand, and sometimes can be driven by actions outside of the individual's control. The stress and pressures of life can have a huge impact on the individual's behaviour and it's important to involve HR where necessary, to support you as a team leader.

SECTION "4"

Communication

Communication is the way express our needs to others, we send and receive messages through communicating with our peers. It is also known as a two way process of reaching a level of understanding between team members. Participants not only exchange information, news, ideas and feelings but also create and share meaning. These can be done face to face or via emails, mails and all others types of communication. Many issues arise in the workplace based on a misinterpretation of communication. In general, communication is a means of connecting people or places, and it has been approved that in all working places, communication is a key function of management across all departments. An organization cannot operate without communication between levels, departments and employees. There are so many types of communication methods used by people across all over the world; verbal communication can be face to face or over the phone, which is known as distance communication. Communication in this day and age within the workplace can be largely reliant on e-mail and social media.

In today's society we all spend a lot of time communicating with others using our phones, computers and face to face, so we all need to develop effective skills on how to communicate face to face. One of the most important skills is the ability to listen and understand the messages. This goes beyond just giving the appearance of attention; we need to be able to adopt the other person's perspective in order to understand fully the message being sent. We need to actively listen, because all meaning resides in the ability to empathise with the individual.

There are plenty of communication barriers that we may face in the workplace. We can be aggressive to each other, invade each other's space and shout at each other. One of the biggest problems is that we don't listen to understand, we listen to reply. On a number of occasions I've witnessed two people engaged in a heated conversation. The thing is that both of them are in agreement of the outcome, but because either of them could not take a step back and actively listening to the other, the communication broke down. I've also seen two individual's in each other's space becoming aggressive towards one another. This can lead to disciplinary action and as a team leader you need to train your staff to try and manage conflict to avoid this happening. Stand back, listen and try to diffuse the situation as well as you can.

Some other barriers which have an impact on communication across all working sectors, is language. The common tongue isn't everyone's first language, and it is important to take this into consideration when communicating with others. As a team leader or a line manager you need to maintain a positive attitude and smile when communicating with others. If you do that, most people are more likely to respond positively to you. No one wants to be around someone who is frequently miserable with a negative attitude. Even when things do not go to plan, stay optimistic and learn from your mistakes. One of the most important parts of a good communicator is to make sure you treat people equally and always aim to communicate on an equal basis. Avoid patronising people, build trust and respect within your team and be an active listener. Listening is a necessary and essential part of the communication process, and it's a way of demonstrating respect for others. Don't talk over people as this will demonstrate a lack of respect. By talking over someone is like you saying '' I am not interested and I don't care what you're saying''. This will really offend people and they will lose respect for you. Always try to actively listen to the other person and don't try to finish their conversation or sentence.

I personally experienced the language problem when I first arrived in England over 44 years ago. I found it very frustrating when trying to hold a conversation with another person, whose first language was English. I found it difficult to answer their questions and listen to them as I couldn't understand what was being said. I arrived in this country with 20 other students from my hometown in Libya, and as we all lived in a guest house we only ever communicated in Arabic. At one stage, I started to think about leaving England and going back to my birth country. However, I've been brought up in a way that enables me to strive towards my goals and to motivate myself to succeed. The fear of falling at the first hurdle made me take a step back and think about what I needed to do to achieve my goal. I made the decision to move out of the guest house into a flat, and started mixing with English people. I made a few friends and tried to learn the language from them. I attended college soon after that and I picked up the language and integrated into the society I was now living in. It is all about the desire to succeed and the self-motivation to achieve your goals. There are other barriers to communication such as the environment, and your perception of other people. This can have an impact on the conversation you may be having with them. If you have preconceived ideas or if you have personal issues about someone, then you will have already formed an opinion about that individual and the communication with that person will break down. Always leave personal feelings as separate as you can, and don't judge people based on your pre-conceptions of them. Judge by their actions, and always make sure that you are aware of other people's emotions. Adopt empathy to your employees that may be struggling, and always maintain eye contact, being sure to use first names where appropriate. Do not be afraid to ask others for their opinions as this will help to make them feel valued. By offering words and actions of encouragement, as well as praise, will make members of your team adopt this approach for everyone. Your team will feel wanted, valued and appreciated as a result of your method of communication. If you let others know that they are valued, they are much more likely to give you their best, it is important to remember that communication with your team is not a matter of one sender and one receiver, rather an exchange in which you and your team members are both senders and receivers. They must be aware of the multicultural society we live in as it can impact on communication with people from different ethnic and cultural backgrounds. It's an enormous challenge for all work places, and some people may find it difficult to integrate into society because of this.

Team Communication

Good team leadership is all about communication. The people who work for you should know exactly what is expected of them. In my experience over the years I have found that I need to make sure that the new member of the team has a very clear understanding of what I am expecting of him/her, and what they need to do to achieve the goals which have been set for them. This must be done on day one and must be monitored by the team leader to ensure the employee is on track. It is really important to get your message across to your team on day one, so they know where they stand. Remember there is only one way to earn respect and that is by being judged on what you say and do.

As a team leader you should provide a high level of communication to your team members about:
- The work place core values
- The expectation behaviours
- The goals and results that have been achieved
- Work place rules and health and safety expectations
- Any goals and requirements that still need to be achieved
- How to achieve these goals
- Where team members can go for support and help

When communicating with your team members, you must use a consultative approach; this entails actively listening to the team member's concerns and opinions before deciding upon appropriate actions. An effective consultative approach also means that you, as team leaders, should provide feedback to your team members on a regular basis. You shouldn't wait for their appraisal time or date as issues may arise long before this time.

I have to admit, that in my early years as a team leader, I could only see and focus on the way I wanted the job to be done. I did not accept other people's ideas or points of view. At the time, I was a poor listener. Over the years I have learned that there are other people who have been in the job longer than me, and they have plenty of experience and good ideas about how the job should be carried out. I have listened and learned from them which have enabled me to achieve the best from my team. Use their experience to your advantage.

As a team leader you need to be a good listener. It is a very powerful tool to have and there is a big difference between listening and active listening. Always focus on active listening instead of passive listening. The difference is that active listening means you engage and respond to the other person based on what they have said; passive listening is simply the act of listening with no response. No one likes communicating with someone who only cares about putting and forcing their own view across and does not take the time to listen to other people. Active listening involves paying close attention to what the other person is saying, asking clarifying questions to assure the other person that they have your full attention, and you understand what is being said. Through active listening, you can respond appropriately as you have fully understood the conversation topic.

In most work places, regardless of the job type, team leaders and managers have a daily meeting or team communication update. Usually in these meeting, the team leader from each department meet with senior managers to report about the previous day's achievements and all the issues faced by the team. They discuss how they can achieve their targets, and as a team leader you must have at hand all the information you need to answer any questions asked about your team. Make sure you give the information that you have, and if you are unsure or don't have the information, tell them that you will get back to them when as soon as you get the information. In my experience, most managers usually have the answer for most questions, as they always do their own preparation before attending meetings. Always be honest and reassure your employee that you will get back to them with the information once you have investigated it. You have been put in the positon as team leader because senior managers have put their trust in you, and you must respect their trust and deliver what is required of you.

Most car manufacturing team leaders and line managers have a daily 10 minute meeting with their team members. This is to go over their achievements over the previous 24 hours, and set their targets for the next 24 hours. Then the team leaders or the line managers report to senior managers during the group meeting. These kinds of shop floor meetings take place in most areas of work. If you are in hospital you will notice the senior members of staff surrounded by a numbers of health care professionals to go through a handover for the patients for the day. This information is fed to the senior doctor and senior nurse for approval. The same can be said about any job. I have witnessed these meetings; I was in the airport early morning last year and I could see all airline desk staff gather together with their team leaders. They were taking instructions and advice about how to handle the customers and what needed to be done to speed up the process of check in. I have seen these kinds of meeting in many airports around the word, and it may only last for 10-15 minutes but it's very important for the staff to have their team leaders or line managers behind them to support and motivate them.

Learn to Listen

Listening is one of the most important components of communication. There is difference between listening and hearing. I have been accused on a number of occasions by my Wife that I am not listening to what she is saying. She may be right (sometimes), as I am hearing her but not always actively listening to her. She may say I have "selective hearing." For example, if I am in the garden I could hear her shouting "football's coming on now," and I usually respond immediately and come inside. But when she shouts to me, to tell me the door handle needs replacing for the 5th time, I don't actively listen meaning the job doesn't get done. I think this is happening to most people, and the reason is because we are not actively listening. We are only hearing what the other person has said, rather than taking in what we need to know. Listening is more important than just hearing or nodding your head whilst you're really daydreaming about what you're going to have for your tea. We need to learn that being an active listening, is also about our non-verbal clues, and how we demonstrate this to the person we are listening to.

Something as simple as asking open ended questions can be a good way of showing that you are actively listening. You could say to someone who is not happy about the feedback you have given them; " I understand that you are not happy about the feedback you have received about your performance, thanks for asking to see me and I appreciate and understand your disappointment. We will try to set a development program to help you improve your performance." Another way of showing you are actively listening is by trying to ask specific questions like '' "How long do you expect your training process to last?" At the same time, try to demonstrate concern by saying "I am happy to help you; I know you are going through some tough challenges while you are trying to complete the project."

E-Mail Communication Problems

I am going to highlight some of the problems people face when using the e-mail system as a way of communication with others, and what can you do to avoid these kinds of issues.

E-mail can create problems for staff, and can lead to criminal convictions in some cases. Poor e-mail communication can lead to confusion and doubt, which can lead to mutual uncomfortable feelings between people and departments. When you are sending an e-mail to pass over a substantial amount of information, it can be difficult for the recipient to understand the content of the message. This will result in the whole message being misunderstood. Keep your e-mails short and straight to the point and make sure that the important information is relayed so any actions are completed.

One of the disadvantages of sending e-mail is the lack of face to face communication. As the recipient cannot hear your tone of voice and can't see your facial expression, it can be difficult for the recipient to understand the true meaning of your message. Sometimes your e-mail may be misinterpreted as rude or aggressive to the recipient, even if this was not your intention. One thing I have learned over the years when replying to e-mail, is to make sure I don't include everyone in the conversations by hitting ''reply all." Not everyone needs to know about the conversation, as it may be sensitive and private. Sharing information that's not yours to share can come with some huge difficulties – never assume that it is ok to share information that's not yours to share in the first place. I've observed employees sending emails in a frantic manner, hitting the keyboard as fast as they can in a fit of rage to one another. What good will this achieves? Nothing. Both of them will become angry over something which could easily have been resolved if they would have both taken a step back from the conversation.

People sometime sending regular e-mails marked as urgent to get your attention. If the email isn't urgent, the recipient will pick up on this 'trick,' and begin to ignore your emails. Unless it is 100% urgent, in my opinion, it should not be marked urgent. In case of urgency an issue may be better resolved by picking up the phone and speaking to the other person. Alternatively if you can try to have a face to face conversation with the individual then that's even better. You must remember at all times, that the tone of your message reflects your relationship with the other person. You need to choose your words very carefully as some people may take offence. Be especially mindful if you work with people from different generations, have language barriers or from different back grounds, social experiences and lifestyles.

One of the most irritating things is when someone sends an e-mail where the subject is not includes. In this case, the sender is forcing the recipient to open the e-mail to figure out what the email about. In today's world we receive a huge numbers of e-mails every day, and we don't have time to read them all. By including the subject the recipient can look at their important e-mails first. Another irritating problem associated with e-mails is when we receive an email with all words in capital letters. IT FEELS LIKE YOU'RE BEING SHOUTED AT. If you are upset or angry, this is not the right way to deal with it. It is OK to draft an email, and then come back to it after a few hours, when you may have calmed down and your perspective may have changed. It will help you accomplish your goal faster because you will be seen as patient and professional as opposed to being sharp and nasty.

Just remember the following steps when you are just about to compose or reply to an e-mail;
- Make sure you send clear accessible emails
- Just take a moment before you send an email. Ask yourself if you should be using emails at all. Is it better to phone or wait until you meet with the person?
- Make sure your email is focused on the point and only copy the people in who need to see the email. Information should be shared on a "need to know basis."
- Any email you send is a reflection on you so remain professional and calm. Imagine how others might interpret the tone of your message, as they can't see you but they can hear you through your emails. Proof read what you send before it is sent.

SECTION "5"

Developing a Vision & Goals

We live in a diverse world, and with that come a variety of different values and beliefs from various backgrounds. We may find that our working place is very diverse and hold various characteristics. If you decide to dedicate your time and energy to this employer and give 100% to the organization, we then need to find out how to work with our team members and work toward the employer goals using the organization core values and visions.

Most companies and organizations all have some kind of values or visions which they use to drive their employees. For example they may focus on team work, results, personal developments, and improvement ideas. All these will help with the growth of the business and provide very good customer satisfaction.

A vision statement is not what the employers or the organization is currently about, but what they strive to achieve. It may be what employees are already doing or what team leaders intend to do, however, it is up to the team leaders to keep it on track and set standards for the group by setting goals. This allows employees to move the organization to a higher level within a given time.

You will need to ask yourself and your team the following questions:-
* Can we change the past? The answer to that is no we cannot change what we have done or what we have achieved.
* Can we change the present? The answer to that is yes we can; we need to set a high standard for our team to achieve, and that will keep everyone working hard to improve the present situation.
* Can we change the future? The answer to that can both yes and no. It depends on how we change and how much we want to change the present.

There are plenty of ways which have been used by lots of working sectors across all types of business to develop a vision for their employers. Here are some of the ones I have used over the years with my team. Brainstorming this will start the creative thinking progress and all team members will be engaged to give their ideas and views. We must remember that there are no 'bad' ideas. We must look at all the ideas before we start to remove them from the list.

In my work place we have a system which has allowed any one to submit their idea; this is known as a continual improvement system. A team of employers will take a look at the improvement ideas and give feedback to the individuals who submitted the idea.

The team must try and avoid working on all the ideas submitted, as this can result on none of the goals being achieved. They should make a list on the idea most feasible for the team to work on, and motivate their team to focus on this.

Five steps to get your team see the same vision as you
- Lead by example
- Inspire a shared vision
- Challenge the process
- Enable others to act
- Encourage the heart

As a team leader you will need to be the driving force behind the improvements you are setting for your team, as they will see you as the role model. If you show them how much you're committed to achieve a set goal, and you challenge the present status, then this will motivate them to achieve their new goals and they will see your vision. Change management is one of the most difficult things to do and it is important to introduce changes in small stages. If you try to enforce all the changes at the same time most likely you will fail to sell your vision and improvement ideas to the team. When you are successfully selling the vision to your team, then you need to let them work on the project and delegate the responsibilities to members of the team. Give them time to take and support them as they work through the improvements or the project.

It's very important to keep the motivation going at the time of improvement. You may get setbacks but work with your team in order to move past these. Keep the focus on the final result and encourage your team to challenge the current process. Look at the final benefits for both the team and the employers.

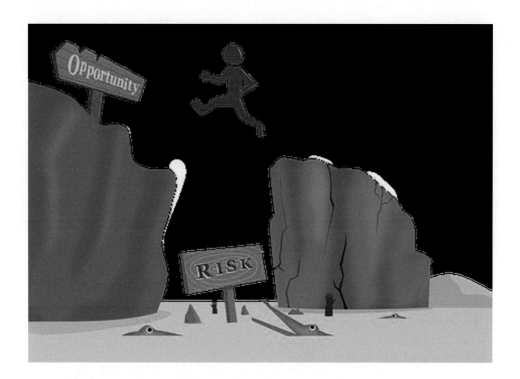

Goal Setting Approach

Goal setting can affect your team and will affect your organization internally as well as externally through its performance. It could affect the organization or service provider, and it will depend on the type of business you are working on. Your team's goals should be relevant to the organization's goals. Team leaders must give team members a clear direction when it comes to goal setting so that your objectives are being met. The employers or the organization's goals should matter to the whole team. This will empower all members to know that what they do is important to the organization's success. The results of such empowerment can increase motivation within the teams and increase a sense of loyalty to the employers.

SMART goals are a good way of setting goals which are achievable and realistic.

SMART usually stands for: -
- Specific
- Measurable
- Attainable
- Realistic
- Timed

Here is an example of what is meant by a SMART goal. As a team leader I want to improve professionally in my position so that I can increase my knowledge and become better at my job. I could ask for a salary increase and my improvement will be measurable against set standards. These standards are relevant to my responsibilities and I will document my progress and work with my manager to ensure I am meeting the goals and expectations on time.

If we look at the word "specific" it means you need to choose a specific goal to achieve not an ambiguous one. For example every year after Christmas, everyone wants to lose weights.

Rather than saying or thinking that you want to have a body like a body building champion of the year, you should be thinking about losing a few pounds to feel healthy. At the same time you should be able to see the weight coming off and that will give you some aspect of your goal that can be measured. This may motivate you to carry on with your goal. Don't fall for the trap by setting impossible goals like losing two stone in a month. After a few months people give up on this type of goal. Make sure you set challenging but achievable goals. Any goals you set must be relevant to your overall plane. To achieve your goal to lose the 10 pounds you have set yourself, then you need to set a time. You can't set a time of seven days to lose 10 pounds as this is not achievable. You have to be realistic about what you can and cannot achieve within the time frame.

So when setting goals for your team make sure you think about the above example. Setting an impossible goal for someone could result in de-motivating the team and they could potentially give up.

Leadership summary

Here is a summary of the key points

- Self-motivation is a key to achieve set goals. The focus must be on the service your work place provides to their customers. This applies to all types of job. If you are a doctor or a nurse then your customer will be your patient. If you are a policeman, then your customer is the public, and so on.
- You must be able to persuade and influence others to carry out the tasks or the jobs using the skills to empower and motivate team members. You must be able to delegate tasks effectively.
- As a leader you need to have the skills to handle pressure and stress by staying calm and in control. Always display a confident and calm personality when under stress. This will make the job easier. You need to be a good planner.
- Leaders need to have good communication skills and must have the ability to express your views clearly. It's vial to have these skills which will lead to strong working relationships with the team. To be able to have these interpersonal skills you need to have good listening skills and be sensitive to people's needs. Your communication with your team and others depends on how good of a listener you are. If you understand what your team and customers want then you will achieve your goal.
- Part of the leadership responsibility is to create a 'no blame' culture, and not to dwell on negative things. Demonstrate a consistently positive attitude to work, just move on and learn from the mistakes and create a coaching culture to develop the team strengths.
- Leaders must be honest with their actions and needs to display sincerity, integrity, and provide sympathy and support when the person is anxious or upset.
- Leadership is about showing fair treatment to all people regardless of their background, work ethic, and religion or where they come from. Be polite and considerate, not arrogant and rude, and treat each member of your team as an individual. You need to remember that prejudice is the enemy of justice.

- Leaders are expected to show creativity by thinking of new and better goals, ideas, and solutions to problems. You must try to be an innovative and show the 'can do' attitude at all times.

SECTION "6"

Team Work

Team work is a group of people working together as a team; this can be in any work sector. If you look at hospital wards you see a number of nurses working together as a team looking after a number of patients. Every one of them may have different responsibilities but they work together as a team to provide the best care. The same can be said about line assembling manufacturing team workers; every one of them are depending on the other to complete each part before the final module is completed and sent to the customers. Every member of the team is known as a team player who is able to get along with his colleagues and peers and work together in cohesive group. Cooperating in a team is a way of establishing and developing a greater sense of collaboration and trust between all team members.

But before we start to look at team work we should ask our self why should we be a team?

In most working organisations, teams are most likely to perform better than the individual. It is also more likely that a team can achieve their employer's goal as a combined effort rather than the sole effort of one individual. As in most cases, not one human can have all the skills of a team. Each member of the team can provide different types of skills, different work ethics, different motivations and different behaviours. All these together can provide the employers with good team skills to provide the service required to achieve the set goals and fulfil the organization mission. It is also a fact when people working together can sustain enthusiasm and motivate each other to achieve their goals.

Team work is the key to any successful team. A few years ago I watched the boat race between Oxford and Cambridge. This kind of sport is 100% dependent on team effort. Usually Cambridge is the underdog. Oxford had won the previous three races, and were sure of them self to win. The team leader of Cambridge motivated his team and when the race started his team listened to his instructions and led themselves to victory. During my holiday in Australia a few years ago I went out with the family for a meal at a restaurant. The place was very busy and I got talking to the manager. I said "it is busy here tonight," he replied "yes it's busy and we are short staffed, but the team have shared the responsibilities and pulled through." I then said, "Can you not just get a replacement for the day by calling the employment office?"

He replies, "we cannot train someone to our standards of service in one day. We have core values and standards and need a good amount of training before employing staff to work here. We strive to deliver the best service at all times."

This clear example demonstrates the importance of good team work, and how this is reflected on by strong team leaders.

Here is another example: During a quick stop over in Dubai airport during a connecting flight, I noticed that the team leader of the cabin crew formed a circle with his team for a brief before the next shift. He encouraged his team to smile, remember their core values, and he is available for support and guidance throughout their shift where needed. A quick ten minutes before a shift can motivate your team for the next 12 hours of their shift.

To have a dream team of workers who can work together and achieve the results required for the business, all that is needed is to have a good team leader. That can only come with experience and training which is very important to achieve the required results.

To have a great team will also depend on the environment. It depends on time and quality of training, and what the team can deliver in terms of skills and capabilities. People learn at different paces to one another, and some may require more support and training as a result of this. If you see potential within an individual that will benefit your team, then it's better to wait for that individual to be fully skilled to carry out the job. Team work is the key to any successful team.

If you can help your team member to become better at what they do and achieve their careers and aspirations, then you will be a good team leader.

Team Building

A good team usually has a productive team which must have members that share common goals; a common vision and idea with some level of interdependence that requires both verbal and physical interaction with others. Teams come into existence because they share the same attitudes and visions about a particular project or a job. They may come together for a number of different reasons; they may be working in the same section or department but their goals are the same. To achieve their best performance and experience success, the end results may differ, but the means by which every team member gets there is the same – teamwork. Every member of the team is accountable when it comes to teamwork.

A team succeeds when its members have the same commitment and self-motivation to achieve the common objectives. Every team member must have defined roles and responsibilities. A good effective communication system between all members is very important. It also depends on good personal relationships between all team members and good working procedures. It's very important to have good team morale in order to be a successful team and these can only be achieved if the team has been supported and has the resources to succeed.

Now we understand how to build a team we need to look at the team work skills. There are many skills required to create a good team to work on a project or to carry out an important task. One of the most important parts of team work is for all team members to be good listeners. As a team member you need to understand what has been said, which means you have to be an active listener and ask questions to ensure you know what your responsibilities are as a member of the team. You also need to respect all your team members' views and ideas.

As a team leader you may find it difficult to control performance standards, as some members of the team find themselves not having the chance to participate in the task or the project. This means as a team leader you need to make sure all team members have responsibilities. If there are dominating members, ask them to step aside and give other team members a chance to participate.

As team leaders or line mangers you need to know what skills each member of the team can bring and contribute to the project. Make sure you choose the correct personalities for the team, people that can accept the views and ideas of others. You need the optimist, the devil's advocate, the person to seek out flaws, the person to facilitate solutions.

Team Development

Team development is a key to the success of any business regardless of its type. Any company must have a team development plan for their employees if they want to achieve their goals and be successful.

So how does team development work? The development of any team can be done in a series of steps as shown on the graph below:-

Success steps

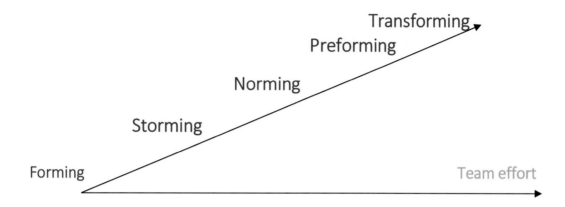

Forming; this is the first stage of forming a team to work together on a project or a solution to resolve an issue or a problem. It is very important as part of the five stages to have a clear vision on what the team should be and how they are going to work together. The team members need different responsibilities in performing the task, otherwise you will end up with a team which will agree on everything and that will not resolve the outstanding issues or problems.

Storming: - At this stage, members of the team may disagree on a number of issues. You will see some conflict and disagreement of opinion between the team members. Some of the team members will become increasingly frustrated and will lose motivation for the task or project. Some of the conflict can be healthy to drive the project forward as long the conflict and disagreement is done in a professional and calm way, and the team are still able to work effectively as a unit.

Norming: - At this stage the team will by now have a clear vision and clear direction on what they need to do to achieve the required results for their projects. You will see as a team leader that the team members become increasingly positive about the team. Morale is high and the team are very motivated to start using their skill as an individual to contribute to the team project.

Preforming: - at this stage each member knows their individual responsibility to the team project, and each one starts to work on the part of the task which they have been tasked with. At this stage the team leader must make sure everyone understands their responsibility and what needs to be done to move the project to the next stage. Feedback from members at this stage is vital as the next stage is to transform the project to actions.

Transforming: - The job is done and transformed to the final stage.

Over the years, I have found that one of the most effective ways to develop any member of my team is to make sure that I give regular feedback to the individual. I know lots of team leaders across all types of jobs find it hard to give feedback, particularly if it is negative. I have found that if I keep giving feedback regularly, and communicate with the individual about their performance, they understand where they are going wrong and they try to improve their skills to achieve a better performance. In my experience I have found that it is better to let the team member knows as soon as I see they are underperforming. You must not wait for the annual appraisal .Take your chance when you see the problem arising – this will prevent it from worsening and sending the team further away from their target.

Team leader's roles in relation to team development

As a team leader you must encourage and maintain open communication with all members of the teams and with other departments and teams who can contribute to your team development. It is imperative to keep department managers on the communication link, as information can be circulated to all people who may be affected by any actions taken.

Your team will be looking at your actions and it's imperative that you set a good example and remain optimistic and open minded. Most of your team members will follow your examples. Your behaviours and actions must be at the highest standards. Always try to look out on the positive things and that will help to motivate and inspires your team to follow your steps. Don't dwell on setbacks, move on and maintain a healthy team dynamic with plenty of encouragement for creativity and risk taking. Make sure you recognize and celebrate the team members' contributions and achievements. It's very important to celebrate the team successes as this will set the standards for others to follow as people like to be rewarded for their contributions. This will encourage more team members to be involved. I know most work sectors think team development and achievements is part of the daily responsibilities for the individual, and this may be correct, but some kinds of reward and encouragement for creativity and achievements can go long ways for businesses achieving their targets.

It's also very important as a team leader to control any bad behaviours and conflict which can occur during team work. You will sometimes see the team members attacking personalities or ideas of other members of the team and constantly criticise others. Some people will display aggressive behaviours and others will act bored and uninterested. As a team leader you will need to act quickly to make sure that all members of the team know that good relationships are a priority. In extreme circumstances some people cause conflict with others and display extreme angers, you will need to deal with this accordingly and professionally.

Team work summary

- Remember the responsibility of team work on any project is to improve the present status and to solve problems arisen from the new improvements.
- Any team put together to work on any project or idea can only be as good as its members. Respecting each other is one of the most important attributes to a good team.
- Maintain good communication links with all team members and others who may have an effect on the outcome of the project or the improvement idea.
- All members of the team must participate and help others to achieve the required results for the team project. Everyone must contribute in some way – big or small.
- The team leader or the project leader must identify any problems or any conflicts which can arise amongst the team members, and try to resolve them in calm way and find ways to make decisions and gain consensus.
- Celebrate success and give recognition to each member of the team on their contributions to the completion of the project.

SECTION "7"

Motivation

This isn't going to be a motivational statement or a speech, instead, I am going to explain what I learned about the science behind how to get motivated in the first place and how to stay motivated for the long-run. Whether you're trying to figure out how to motivate yourself or how to motivate a team, it is important that you pay attention.

What is motivation?

Motivation is made up of internal and external factors that stimulate desire and energy in people to be continually interested and committed to a job, role or subject, or to make an effort to attain a goal.

If we take a look at John McEnroe, one of the greatest players in the history of tennis, his internal motivation is to be number one in the world of tennis and to eliminate the achievements of Bjorn Borg, and many more before him. His external motivation is to win as many grand slam cups as possible and reap the financial rewards. He had the desire to be the best at that sport, which also motivated him to be determined and committed to the pursuit of his goal. The external factor is the outcome of wining the grand slam and to be the best in the world. There are many business men and women who had the motivations and the desire to build their own business empires from nothing. Their internal motivation factors were; they don't want to settle for working for someone and accept low pay for the rest of their life. Perhaps they have seen their parents struggle to make ends meet, with low pay and long working hours. This could have been an internal motivation to do better for themselves and their family. The external motivation for them were the achievements of their hard work which resulted in building a successful business and finically were rewarded very well which helped to secured their family futures.

Self-Motivation

Self-motivation is the desire and the ability to do something without any influence from other. It's what makes us push ourselves to the limit to achieve our goals or objectives. Sportsmen and women have the ability to push themselves to the limit in order to be their very best.

The Psychology of what motivates us

Motivation is what causes us to take action to satisfy our needs, hopes and ambition. Whether it is taking driving lessons to be able to pass the driving test, or going to drama school to become an actor or actress, the individual will be highly motivated if they want to achieve their goals.

Why it is important to be motivated

Motivating your team is vital to any business, a motivated team (workforce) means highly productive staff, all which will help the company and any business sectors to achieve the business goals. This should be one of the main objectives for any team leader to maintain the success of the business.

Now we understand the Psychology of what motivates us and why we need to be motivated we need to start to look how we are going to get everyone motivated and sustain the good factors to keep all employees motivated. There are many ways for the employers to get their employees on the right track and motivate them to achieve the results required to meet the customers' needs. Many people and employers believe that if they pay the employees more money they will become motivated. This is true in some cases but not every time and it may only work for a short period of time. A lot of people prefer to come to work in pleasant and friendly environments with the clear direction on their responsibilities and opportunities for self-development. They want to help to develop their skills to achieve promotions within set times. My advice to team leaders is that you should provide every opportunity in your control or within your abilities to your team to develop. Never give any promises out of your control; don't promise them a pay rise as this is not under your control. You can put recommendations forwards for promotions when the opportunities become available, but it is always difficult for the team leader or the line manager when they see their team members do everything possible and when they may not be successful in getting the promotion they want. As a team leader you must support the individual to keep going.

Ways of implanting motivation

By letting your team be part of the planning and problem solving process can have a number of effects on the way they behave. People who are part of a decision making process become the owners of it. I have found that is very important as I have a lot of experience dealing with team work. One thing that kept my team motivated, was allowing them their own responsibilities for the job and letting them play a big part of the decision making process for their department. As an example, when installing a new machine or a new work bench in the area where that a specific team are based, it is very important to take their view. After all, they are the ones who are going to be using the new machine. These kinds of issues occur all time in most factories and in all business sectors. The decision is usually taken by a member of the management team and the team workers who are using the equipment haven't been consulted. To be a successful business you need to motivate your team to drive the process forwards.

Always try to promote ownership and involve your team members in the design and implementation of the change or idea. From my experience, I know that most people just want to come to work, do their job, and go home. They haven't been involved in the changes or improvements being made to their working area, as the original planning processing have been implemented by senior managers. In my opinion, any changes being implemented in a workplace should be discussed with all team members, and everyone should have the opportunity to contribute. At the end of the day, these are the people who are going to be operating the equipment, so they should be involved in the decision making process. This will positively influence their motivation and happiness within their role, which will ultimately drive success for the business.

One of the most demotivating factors in any working environment, regardless of the business type, is that we always reflect on what we have not achieved rather than what we have. We tend to pick out the negative points which can be detrimental to the business. At the end of each working day, a team leader should reflect on what the team has achieved in that day. You as the team leader should praise your team for their achievements and "sandwich" any constructive criticism. For example; "You achieved your targets today and performed really well. If you could try and work on time management tomorrow then that may take us over our desired targets, but overall well done for today." This will keep them motivated whilst also knowing what their goals are for the next shift. If you want your department or company to achieve success then positive reassurance can go a long way in motivating your team. Next time you are on the shop floor, try to show some kind of appreciation and you will see how this influences your team; it will drive them to achieve more. This is something a number of working industries and service sectors fail to do. This has a huge impact on their business and when this happens, most workers will do what they can or as little as they and go home after work with no real praise or reward. You must give regular feedback on their performance every week; good and bad. The team needs to put their poor performances behind them, and focus on improving their performance for the future. Build people's confidence in the strategic direction of the team and create a positive image of the leadership's capability within the shift. Always help individuals to feel positive about their own contribution and always try to instil a sense of pride in others about the work they do. This can only happen if you set examples for the team. If you are a team leader who doesn't show a sense of pride and self-motivation in your achievements, then your team will follow this same example. Make sure that you show a huge sense of pride in your work and your achievements, and your team will follow in your footsteps.

You must always remember the core values of the business, and vocalise this to your team. The focus needs to be on the needs of the customer and the business requirements. This can be different daily depending on the type of business or the service provided and you have to get your team to believe in their capability to deliver outstanding results. This is another important key to having a successful and productive team. You will need to have training programmes for your team so they can be capable of achieving the business and the customer's needs.

One of the key elements in keeping your team fully motivated is by leading and acting in a way which drives the team forward. This can be achieved just by being there with your team. If your team don't see you and don't hear from you daily then their performance will be below standards. Always try to provide a clear sense of direction; as team leader you must set the direction and coach your team to perform in this way. Most people will perform very well when they are confident in their job responsibilities and you must respond promptly to requests and feedback from your team. This is important in maintaining trust within your team.

One of the most surprising things about motivation is that it often comes after starting a new behaviour, not before. For example if you stared to go the gym and frequently run to lose weight and get fit, you will find that you are more motivated once your fitness starts to improve. You will find yourself more motivated to eat healthy and go to the gym because you now have a strong desire to do so. People can often become motivated after listening to a motivational speech, or reading an inspirational book about how to lose weight and get healthier, but active inspiration is a far more powerful motivator. If you have a friend that accompanies you to the gym, you well get motivated by just following their steps. This is known as active inspiration.

Because motivation usually comes as the result of an action being taken by the individual or a group of people, getting started, even in a very small way, is a form of active inspiration that naturally produces improvements within an individual or group. Medical professionals believe that a lack of motivation is often linked to a lack of physical movement. Think about your mind and physical conditions. If you are feeling depressed, bored, or unmotivated and you are not currently engaging in any physical activities, you will effectively feel worse; like a vicious cycle. If you get moving, keeping your mind and body active, then you will most likely feel more motivated by the action that you have taken. If you and your team members want to achieve the best results and highest standards possible, then you and your team need to not only be committed to being motivated to achieve your team mission, but also motivated to getting the job accomplished by going over and beyond.

How to Stay Motivated for the Long-Run

Imagine you are playing a sports game. If you try to play a serious match against your young child, you will quickly become bored. The match is too easy and usually you will let your child win the game as you don't want to upset them. On the opposite end of the spectrum, if you try to play a serious match against a professional football player or a professional sportsman, you will find yourself demotivated for a different reason. The match is too difficult because you know that you are up against the professional. Try to compare these experiences to playing a game of tennis against someone who is your equal in terms of physicality and fitness. As the game progresses, you win a few points and you lose a few points. You have a chance of winning the match, but only if you really try. Because you are fully focused on the game and fully motivated you now have a chance of winning the game. In general, most human beings love challenges as long as they have the chance of achieving their desired results. Over the years, various studies of human behaviour have found that any task which is below our current abilities can be found boring and may discourage the individual to complete the task. But tasks that are right on the border of success and failure are incredibly motivating to our human brains. This can be applied to most types of jobs. If you always do the same work in the same way every day, and you're comfortable with this then that's fine. Eventually though, you will become bored and lose your motivation. Any changes to your daily routine, regardless of how small these changes are, can boost your motivation. If you start to push yourself outside of your comfort zone, you will feel inspired to do more and achieve your goals. If you go to the gym and do the same workout every day I am sure that at some point you will become bored and you will be looking for a new challenge to keep you motivated. Always encourage your team to push their skills and performance levels to a new standard with new challenges. You can get your team to be involved in new projects or activities which will help everyone to stay motivated for a longer time. If you make a list of tasks or jobs you are going to do then tick off each one you complete, you will get extra motivation from your team from knowing they have achieved a task. Another key motivating factor which can keep you and your team motivated for a long time is feedback. This can sometimes be scary but it can also be incredibly motivating. If a member of your team has done well, then the feedback you give them about their performance can serve as an ego boost and motivator. At the same time, constructive criticism can be used to push the individual to do better. Always put your energy, efforts and focus on the things you can control. Forget about those uncontrollable things and remove them from your mind as focusing on them could impede you and your team's progress.

SECTION "8"

Accountability & Delegation

The way I'm going to explain to you what accountability and delegation both mean, is through a personal example. In the department where I work we have four team leaders all working on rotating shifts. During a team leaders meeting with our department managers, a task was put on the table to be carried out by any one of the team leaders who were present at the meeting. No one took responsibility to carry out the job but everyone assumed that someone would do it. Anybody could have done it, but nobody did. The meeting finished and everyone moved on to carry on with their own responsibilities. However, because no one felt that they were accountable for the task raised during the meeting, no one carried it out. This is a clear example of when no one takes accountability for a simple task. It also demonstrates poor communication between all team members. Try to imagine a doctor giving clear instruction to a group of nurses about a vital injection needed for a patient. If no one took accountability to carry out the doctor's instruction, the end result could be fatal. This shows that taking responsibility and being accountable for the task, is an important part of the job. As a team leader, clear communication and clear instruction is very important for people to carry out tasks efficiently and effectively. If you are going to delegate a job to a member of your team, first you need to understand what delegation is and when it is appropriate. Delegation is the assignment of a job or responsibility and accountability is required to achieve the required results. It is one of the most important skills a leader develops in becoming an effective manager.

Now we are going to look to why people don't delegate jobs and tasks to other members of the team. I have to accept that I was one of those people who never delegated. In my early years of the job I liked to take control and do the job myself. I started as an engineer and I was responsible for fixing mechanical issues in the workplace. Now I'm a team leader I still have the same mentality as when I was an engineer. I thought I could do it better than any members of my

SECTION "9"

Conflict

What is Conflict? Conflict is generally defined as a relational dispute between two or more parties. Conflict is a normal part of any healthy relationship and in most working places two people can't be expected to agree on everything, all the time. It is important that we deal with conflict in a calm way rather than just avoiding it. If you agree about everything then that can cause conflict in itself. When conflict is mismanaged, it can cause great harm to a relationship between employees in the work place. Conflict at home between families can lead to break downs in family life. Some people lose their temper quicker than others, but when handled in a respectful, positive way, conflict can provide an opportunity to strengthen the bond between two people. By learning these skills for conflict resolution, you can keep your personal and professional relationships strong and growing.

Every one of us faces conflict on a daily basis, at home, with neighbours, service providers, at work and commercially. We have all discovered that such conflict always costs us emotionally, and may cost us financially. Just take a moment and look back on a phone call to one of the service providers you may have come across in your life. How long did they make you wait on the phone before answering your query? You may lose your temper in this situation, but in my experience it is better to try to be calm and to resolve the issue to achieve the results you wanted. Just remember that resolving such conflicts or disagreement feels good and is good! Yet we have all discovered just how difficult trying to be calm in a situation like this is.

Conflict will always be present in the workplace and it's important to seek resolution, not just to contain the issues and forget about them.

There are two kinds of workplace conflict: - when people's ideas, decisions or actions relating directly to the job are in opposition, or when two people just don't get along. The latter is often called a personality clash; disagreeing with others is not always a negative or destructive process. If it is handled correctly it can lead to a healthy sharing of ideas and opinions and can ideally allow us to accommodate new concepts. This will motivate people to share their views and feelings. Conflict is part of our everyday life and it usually arises out of disagreements with others about how we should behave/act or even think and feel. Without it, we would not challenge each other to do or be better but would merely passively accept what is dished out to us, like robots! From my experience over the years and from what I have seen in the work place, conflict is not the problem but it is how people choose to deal with it that brings us negative results and relationships. Conflict will always exists in every organization regardless of the job type, and to a certain extent indicates a healthy exchange of ideas and creativity. On the other hand, counter-productive conflict can result in employee dissatisfaction, which will reduce productivity, and provide poor service to customers. It can also lead to absenteeism and increased work pressures which can increase stress levels within the environment.

What are the signs of conflict?

Some signs of conflict will be very visible and can be seen when two people have a heated exchange between them. It could be if you are in a meeting and two employees have a disagreement that turns into a stand-off. However, not all forms of conflict are so obvious and can't be seen by everyone in every work organization. Some individuals will always try to hide their feelings as a way of coping with a problem and a way of hiding their weaknesses, and usually they cut them self-off from the team. While a team might react to pressure by cutting itself off from the rest of the organisation, this is something all team leaders and managers must sort out before the problem escalates out of control. Before conflict develops, usually an employee is unhappy about something or may be reluctant to work with another colleague. Productivity may slow down and morale may dip. Behaviour will change and the employee may make unfair comments about another employee which can lead to problems with absence and a willingness to work.

Who is in conflict?

Conflict tends to fall into two broad categories:-

Conflict at work can be between individual employees who may have concerns with another particular employee. Their poor behaviours could be a clash of personalities or may be difference of opinions which could be causing difficulties at work. The other conflict category is the conflict between teams or large groups of employees and management.

Conflict between work colleagues can often lead to accusations of bullying or harassment. Good team leaders should always be ready to talk to both parties involved in conflict and always try to create a climate of open and positive dialogue. If your team member feels able to approach you at an early stage, then problems can often be 'nipped in the bud' before they become formal grievances. It will save time, money and stress further down the line, for both the employer and employees, and will stop the situation developing into a full-blown dispute. You must remember that poorly handled or unresolved conflict can result in poor relationships between individuals and some may hold resentment. It can also lead to ill health for everyone involved.

The most common types of conflict in work place

- **Interdependence Conflicts**

These types of conflict happen when a person relies on someone else's co-operation, output or input in order for them to get their job done. You can see this type of conflict arise in most manufacturing companies, where a conveyor belt operation is in progress. Every step of the process is depending on the one before; if one step is missed by the individual then the next operation cannot be completed and that can cause conflict between the two employees involved in the process.

- **Differences in Style**

An individual may have a preferred way of getting a job done which can differ to another person's preference; this can cause conflict to arise. One person may be task orientated and more hands on, whilst the other is more person orientated, and concerned around everyone having a say in the completing of the task.

- **Differences in characteristics**

Conflict can arise between people because of differences in age, gender, culture and experiences. Team leaders must take to account that some of these characteristics may affect the speed at which the job is completed. This can cause conflict between staff.

- **Personality Clashes**

Personality clashes are usually ignited by people's emotions and perceptions about somebody else's motives and character. Just by saying to someone "you're late again, you're always late" can feel as though they are being targeted. This can cause conflict to arise.

Performance-Review Conflicts

No employee likes to receive a negative performance review, but giving negative feedback in a review can be unavoidable based on the employee's own actions during the review period. Some people may become angry over not receiving expected appraise, and may lash out by spreading discontent through gossip and a negative attitude at work. It's very important to start any performance review by highlighting the good thing first, and then try to find the reason for the other missed chances for improvement. Try to set a time-bound action plan to improve his/her performance

Discrimination Issues

Discrimination can be a source of heated conflict, potentially ending in legal trouble for everyone involved. Discriminatory conflicts can arise from personal prejudices on the part of employees, or perceptions of mistreatment of employees. Discrimination involves protected characteristics such as gender, age, religion, culture etc. You must treat everyone with the same respect, and adopt a zero tolerance attitude towards discrimination in your workplace.

Conflict Resolution Rules

- **Make sure that good relationships are a priority**. Treat the other person with respect. Do your best to be courteous, and to discuss matters constructively.
- **Separate people from problems.** Recognize that, in many cases, the other person is not "being difficult" – real and valid differences can lie behind conflicting positions. By separating the problem from the person, you can discuss issues without damaging relationships.
- **Listen carefully to different interests.** You'll get a better grasp of why people have adopted their position if you try to understand their point of view.
- **Listen first, talk second.** You should listen to what the other person is saying before defending your own position. They might say something that changes your mind.
- **Set out the "facts."** Decide on the observable facts that might impact your decision, together.
- **Explore options together.** Be open to the idea that a third position may exist, and that you might reach it jointly.

SECTION "10"

Barriers

We all face barriers in our working life. Barriers can be anything that hinders the individual or team from achieving their ambition. Some barriers can be out of our control and in these situations, everyone must work together to overcome these barriers. People can be reluctant to accept changes due to being so used to their current way of working. I have seen issues over the years many times, over people unable to accept changes in the workplace. They may be worried about losing control over their job and this can make the process of change difficult in the workplace. Communication can be a big issue when people don't speak the same language, and there are other barriers which can have an impact. Physical barriers and age can limit people from achieving their goals which can then lead to emotional barriers. Before we start to think about how to remove these barriers, we need to develop a successful strategy or method for change. We need to understand the types of barriers that we are faced with. Years of experience in dealing with people in my job, has brought me to the conclusion that it is possible to develop methods in overcoming these barriers, especially when trying to implement any new ideas. I found that not everybody likes change; they are in their comfort zone and are reluctant to stepping out of it. It is essential to identify the gap between recommended practice and current practice and ideally this assessment will also help to identify the potential and actual barriers to change.

How to overcome these barriers

I found over the years that the best way to try to remove barriers is to get people involved. One of the best ways of doing that is by brainstorming, as it's the best way of developing creative solutions to a problem and everyone can offer opinions. It is easy to do and generates lots of ideas. It helps to engage people in the progress of change. We could also use a questionnaire sheet which will help to get clear picture of current practice and provides the opportunity to highlight the need for change through communication of the results. Another way of trying to understand the barriers and remove them is to have a focus group within the team. This will enable a group of people to share ideas and will encourage new ideas and perspectives. It will also help to get people engaged in the change process.

We must remember that there is no one method to overcome all the different barriers. Different approaches will be effective for different people and different situations. Personality clashes between the individual can negatively impact the team and create further barriers to the desired outcome. If you take a look at a team of 25 people who work in the same room and on the same team, you may find that some of them have their own agenda and they are unwilling to compromise for the good of the team and the company. This can become one of the biggest barriers to developing an efficient team. One of the barriers we all face sometimes is the lack of confidence, and you can see this amongst a number of people when they are trying to carry a task without the necessary experience.

SECTION "11"

Time Management

Time management is an essential part of being a team leader. You must invest your time in the job to maximise the results and potential, whilst simultaneously controlling the amount of time spent on each task or specific activity. This is important in increasing effectiveness, efficiency and productivity. It is a very important process which is aimed at managing your time to help with achieving your goals and your priorities. The key to good time management is to delegate some of your responsibilities to your team members. Time management is an effective tool which will help you to stay on top of all activities at work and home. You must be disciplined to achieve good time management and it shouldn't take extreme effort to set up and follow. Here are some the benefits of time management:-

- Less time waste. We all waste a lot of time because we don't set a plane in place and follow it. If you have a set of activities to do in a certain amount of time, and you stick to it, then you will find plenty of time to do other things.
- Less stress and life pressure. If you manage your time correctly then you will not be running around like a headless chicken trying to do everything. Not just in work but also at home. You see people rushing from one place to another trying to get things done and it only adds stress to our lives.

Benefits of Time management

How to manage your time

- **Make a list.** The important thing to remember when making lists is that you actually have to use them. You may want to set reminders on your phone and computer, but you have to be self- disciplined to carry out all tasks as per your time management list. I know that effective lists really do work as I use them regularly. I always try to set a list which I can achieve within the time limits.

- **Set deadlines.** It's very important to stick to the deadline and not keep pushing the task further away from your reach. Try to set the deadline a few days before the task has to be completed, this allows for the possibility that other things will get in the way, but also will allow for you to still get the task done within the deadline.
- **Stop multi-tasking.** We all try to be multitaskers. It's not always the most productive or efficient route. We are human and we usually work better when we are focussed and concentrate on one thing.
- **Delegate responsibilities.** For those of us who like to be in control, the very thought of this is likely to provoke a bit of anxiety. The truth of the matter is that no matter how good we are, we can't do everything. Sometimes we take on more than we can handle or we are given more than we can handle, but this is where we delegate. Delegation is not a sign of weakness, but a sign of intelligence. Use competent, reliable members of the team and share some of the responsibilities. I am sure this will allow you to be less stressed and more productive, with more time on your hands to do other important things. Remember delegation is not that you are running away from your responsibilities, but is an important skill required as a strong team leader.

The key to good time management is to understand the difference between urgency and importance. When you have been given an urgent task or a job to carry out it usually demand your immediate attention, but whether you actually give it your full attention is dependent on how urgent the task is. It is important to prioritise our workload, and weigh up which tasks need completing in which order.

As a team leader or line manager you should be focused, and concentrate on the most important activities or tasks. As we all know dealing with too many urgent tasks can be stressful, so always try to reduce the number of urgent jobs or tasks and try to delegate where you can.

Printed in the United States
By Bookmasters